F**k Trump
2024

4 MORE
YEARS!

Blue wave

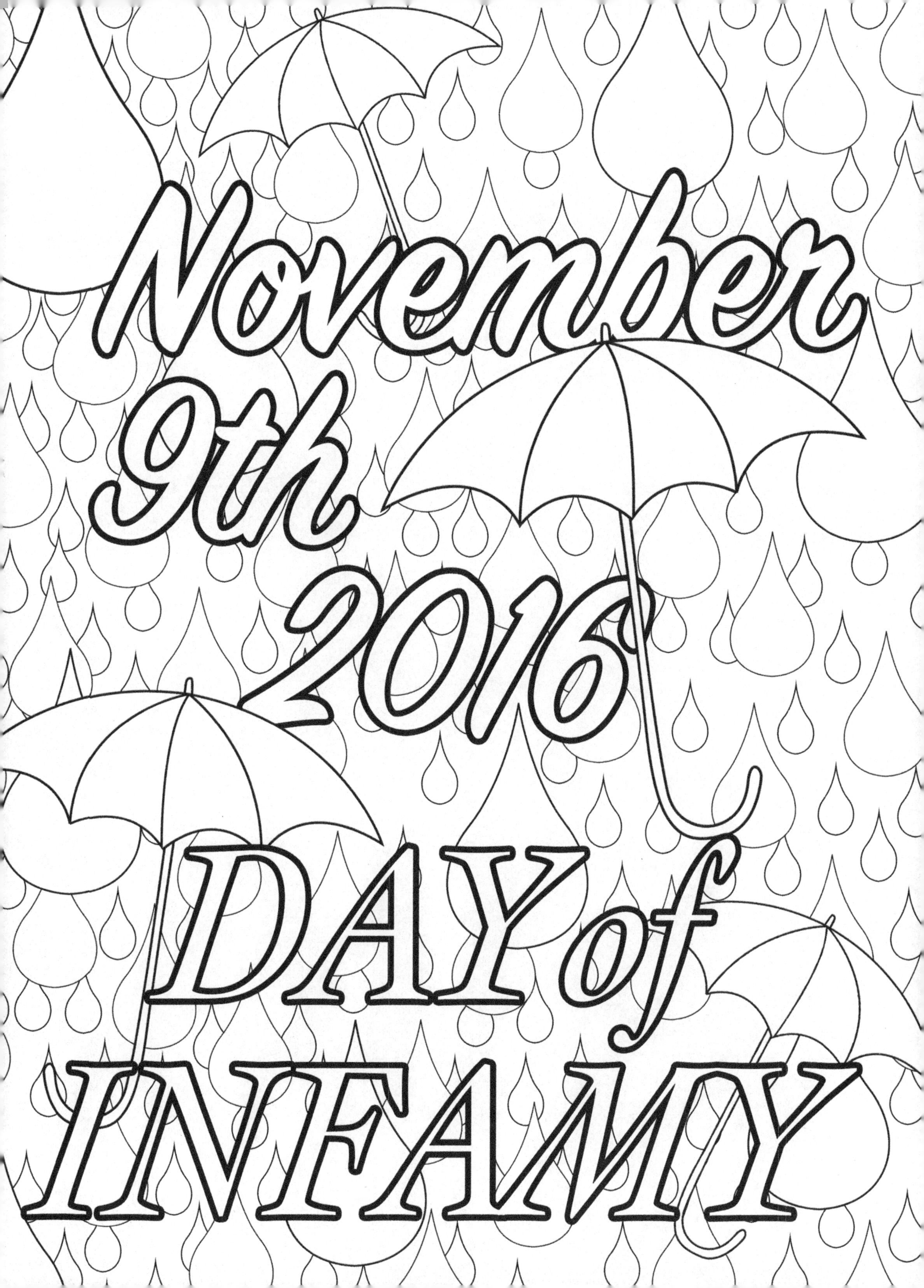
November 9th 2016
DAY of INFAMY

17
76
NEVER FORGET
JANUARY 6TH 2021
INSURRECTION

#Resist

F**K
TRUMP

KAMALA HARRIS
1ST FEMALE
VICE PRESIDENT
YASS!

IMPEACH AGAIN
(if he's re-elected)
3rd Time's a Charm!

Lock HIM up!!!
SHERIFF
FULTON COUNTY
SHERIFF'S OFFICE
PATRICK LABAT
Hillary was supposed to be the one Locked Up!
NOT ME!!

Hildawg
PROUD "Nasty Woman"

Was Not
My President

F**K
TRUMP!

FOREVER
Impeached

FOREVER
MY QUEEN
NOTORIOUS
RBG

GET
WOKE

F**K
TRUMP

#RESIST
#RESIST
#RESIST

STILL MISS YOU

F**K
TRUMP
F**K
TRUMP
F**K
TRUMP
F**K
TRUMP
F**K
TRUMP
F**K
TRUMP
F**K
TRUMP
F**K

NEVER
My President

CK TRUMP
RUM
CK T UMP
MP F CK T
F K TRUM P
CK TRUM P F
F CK TRUM P
CK T UMP F
CK TRUM P

DON'T MESS
with
the
SQUAD

STAY WOKE

#Resist
#RESIST
#RESIST
#RESIST
#RESIST

#RESIST
#RESIST

I CANNOT #RESIST!

I love you.
I know.
F**K TRUMP